CHEMICAL CHANGES

Design	Cooper · West
Editor	Margaret Fagan
Researcher	Cecilia Weston-Baker
Illustrator	Louise Nevett
Consultant	J. W. Warren Ph.D. Formerly Reader in Physics Education, Department of Physics, Brunel University, London, U.K.

Designed and produced by
Aladdin Books Ltd
70 Old Compton Street
London W1

First published in the
United States in 1986 by
Gloucester Press
387 Park Avenue South
New York NY 10016

ISBN 0-531-17032-2

Printed in Belgium

Library of Congress Catalog
Card Number: 86-80625

SCIENCE TODAY

CHEMICAL CHANGES

Kathryn Whyman

GLOUCESTER PRESS
New York · Toronto · 1986

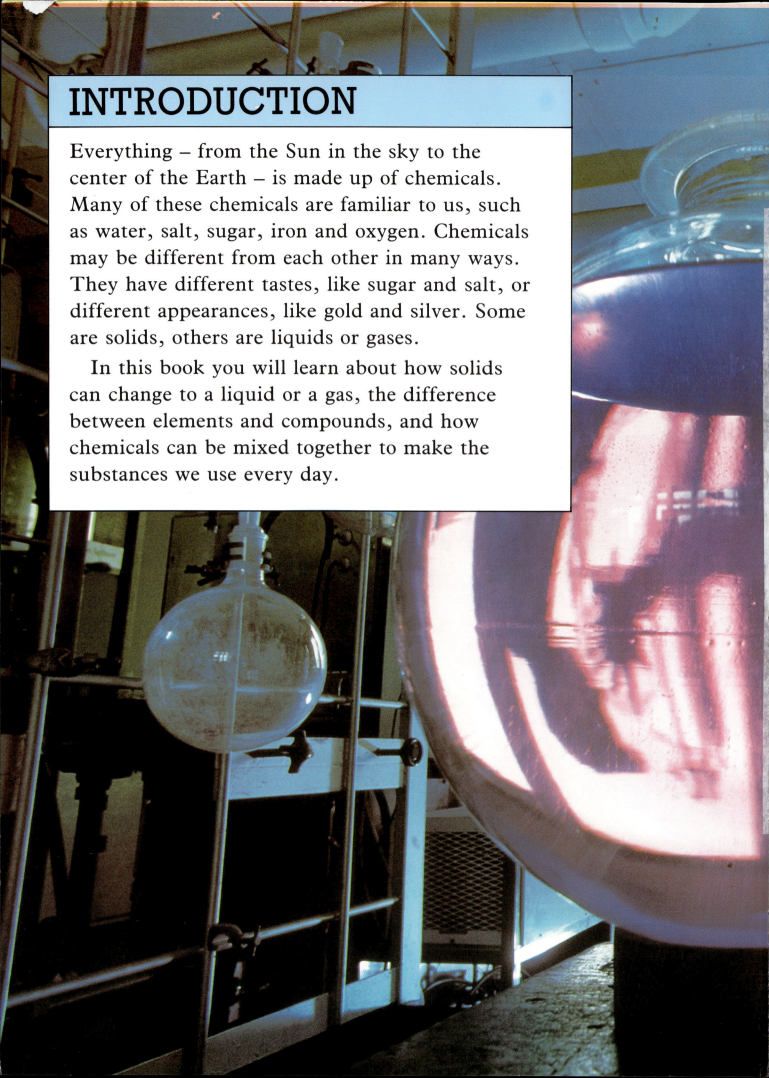

INTRODUCTION

Everything – from the Sun in the sky to the center of the Earth – is made up of chemicals. Many of these chemicals are familiar to us, such as water, salt, sugar, iron and oxygen. Chemicals may be different from each other in many ways. They have different tastes, like sugar and salt, or different appearances, like gold and silver. Some are solids, others are liquids or gases.

In this book you will learn about how solids can change to a liquid or a gas, the difference between elements and compounds, and how chemicals can be mixed together to make the substances we use every day.

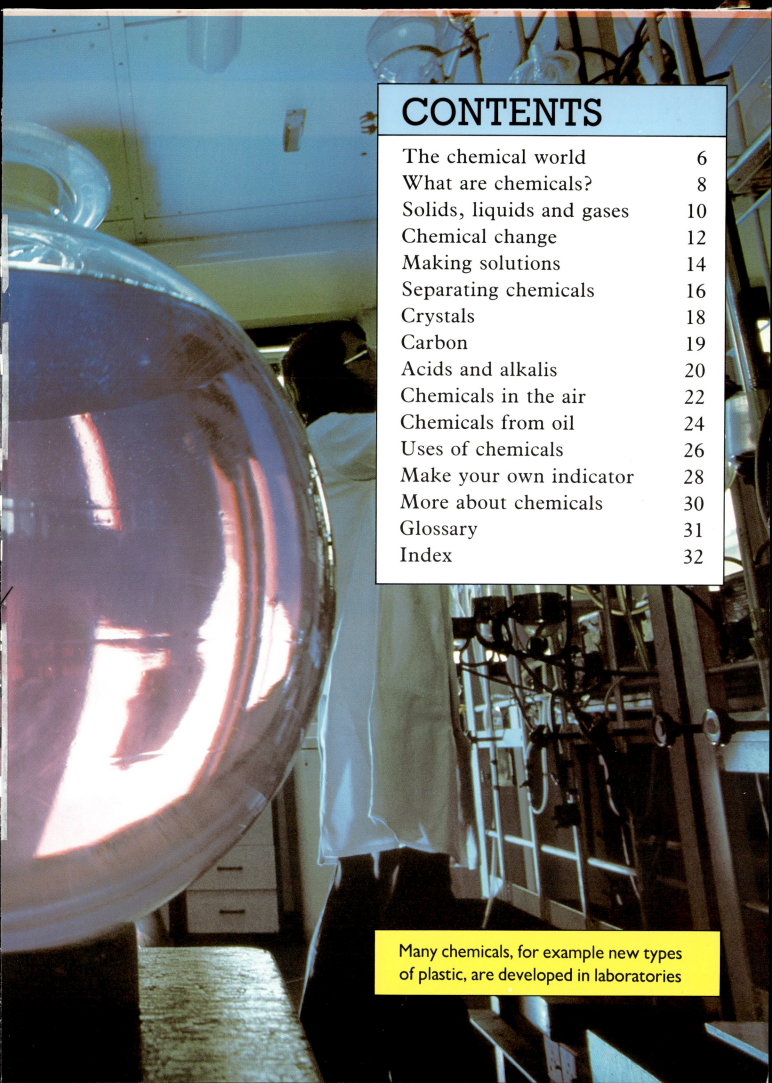

CONTENTS

Many chemicals, for example new types of plastic, are developed in laboratories

Our world is made up of thousands of different substances. We call these substances "chemicals." Chemicals make up the air we breathe, the ground we walk on and the food we eat. Even our bodies are only a collection of chemicals!

Every chemical has its own name. We often put chemicals into groups. Water, salt, sugar and oxygen are all chemicals. We call them "natural" chemicals. Plastics, detergents and cosmetics are everyday chemicals too. But these do not occur naturally – they are "manmade."

Both types of chemicals may be useful. For example, manmade cleaning agents remove all kinds of dirt from our clothes. Natural dyes from plants can be used to color beautiful carpets.

Most of the cleaning agents we use are manmade

Wool and cotton can be dyed with chemicals from plants and dried in the heat

WHAT ARE CHEMICALS?

There are about 100 special chemicals called "elements." They cannot be broken down into simpler chemicals. The gases oxygen and hydrogen are both elements; so are iron and gold. Every element is made up of tiny particles called "atoms," which are much too small to see, even with a microscope. Oxygen is made up of oxygen atoms, iron is made up of iron atoms. Sometimes atoms join together to make "molecules."

Combining chemicals

When two elements combine, they often make a compound that is very different from either of them. The element sodium is a shiny metal. The element chlorine is a green and poisonous gas. Sodium atoms and chlorine atoms can combine to make a very familiar compound – salt! However, we do not make the salt we eat by combining sodium and chlorine. The photograph opposite shows salt being produced from sea water. In cooler countries, salt is mined from underground.

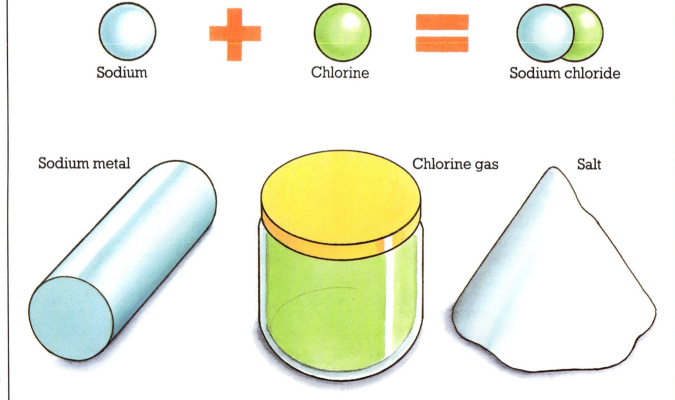

Sodium + Chlorine = Sodium chloride

Sodium metal   Chlorine gas   Salt

A molecule of an element is made up of only one type of atom. But the atoms of one element may join up with the atoms of another element. When this happens a completely different chemical is formed. For example, when two hydrogen atoms join with an oxygen atom, they make a molecule of water. Chemicals that are made from two or more elements combining are known as "compounds." Water is a compound. Sugar, salt, plastics – in fact, most of the chemicals around us – are compounds.

In hot countries, salt is produced from sea water

SOLIDS, LIQUIDS AND GASES

Chemicals may be solids, liquids or gases. Water is a liquid. But if water is cooled to below 0°C (32°F), it freezes and forms ice, a solid. And if it is heated to 100°C (212°F), it boils and changes to steam (water vapor). We say that water can change its "state."

A chemical's state depends on its temperature. Solids may turn to liquids and gases and then back to solids again, as the temperature rises and then falls. We usually see metals, such as gold, in their solid state. But if gold is heated over a flame, it becomes softer and if it is heated to a high enough temperature, it suddenly melts and becomes a liquid. The liquid gold can then be shaped by pouring it into molds. Once the gold cools, it changes back to a solid.

Ice
Because the molecules in a solid, such as ice, are held tightly together and can only move around a fixed point, it has a definite shape.

Water
As a liquid, water molecules can move around more freely. The "shape" of the water depends on the container.

Water vapor
The molecules now move freely in all directions, spreading further apart until they fill their container.

Liquid gold is poured into ingots

CHEMICAL CHANGE

When water changes its state, its molecules are still made of hydrogen and oxygen – the chemical itself has not really changed. But when elements combine to make a compound, new molecules are formed. We call this a "chemical change."

We see examples of compounds forming every day. Most metals combine with chemicals in the air. Copper roofs slowly turn green as the copper combines with water and oxygen to form a new compound. An iron nail left outside soon starts to turn brown and crumbly. The iron has reacted with water and oxygen in the air to form "rust." Cars are made of several metals including iron. They have to be coated in special paints and other chemicals to prevent them from rusting. But eventually oxygen and water find their way through the layers of paint.

When you bake a sponge cake, you start by mixing the different ingredients. Some ingredients, such as flour, are a mixture of chemical compounds. When the cake mixture is heated in the oven, chemical changes, or reactions, take place. From the original ingredients, a new mixture of many different compounds is produced.

Rust is formed when iron reacts with water and air

13

MAKING SOLUTIONS

A teaspoon of salt seems to disappear in a glass of water. But a sip of the liquid tells you that the salt is still there – you can taste it. So what has happened to the salt?

When salt is mixed with water, the sodium and chlorine atoms break away from each other and move freely in the water. Gradually, the sodium and chlorine atoms and the water molecules are mixed up evenly. There are many more water molecules in the solution than atoms of sodium and chlorine. The liquid is called a salt "solution." The salt has "dissolved."

Many solids dissolve in water. Water is a good "solvent." Some substances dissolve in different solvents. For example, paint dissolves in turpentine. Detergents "help" water to dissolve oil, and are often added to soap powders.

Diffusion

If orange juice is poured carefully down a straw into a glass of water, an orange layer can be seen at the bottom of the glass. The molecules of both the water and the orange juice are moving all the time. Eventually, the orange molecules are spread evenly throughout the water and the solution looks pale orange all over. We call this spreading of molecules "diffusion."

Detergent can be used to clean sea birds damaged by oil pollution

SEPARATING CHEMICALS

There are many mixtures of chemicals in our world. The air is a mixture of gases and dust; the ocean is a mixture of salt and water – a gigantic salt solution! Sometimes we need to separate these chemicals from each other.

One way of separating chemicals is to use a "filter." A face mask is a type of filter. It is made of material that is full of tiny holes. Air can pass through these holes but particles of dust or paint are too big and get trapped on the outside of the mask.

A filter would not help to separate salt from a salt solution. The sodium and chlorine atoms and the water molecules which form a salt solution are small enough to pass through the holes of any filter. But if the solution is warmed, the water begins to change into steam and eventually only salt is left behind. We call this process "evaporation."

Evaporation

When you swim in the ocean, your body becomes covered with sea water (or salt solution). Later, when you lie on the beach, the heat of the Sun warms this solution. The water evaporates leaving salt on your skin.

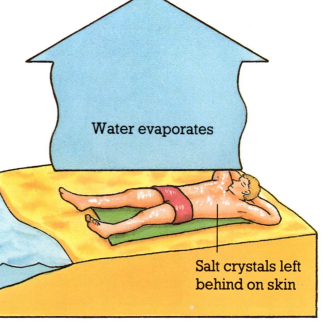

Water evaporates

Salt water

Salt crystals left behind on skin

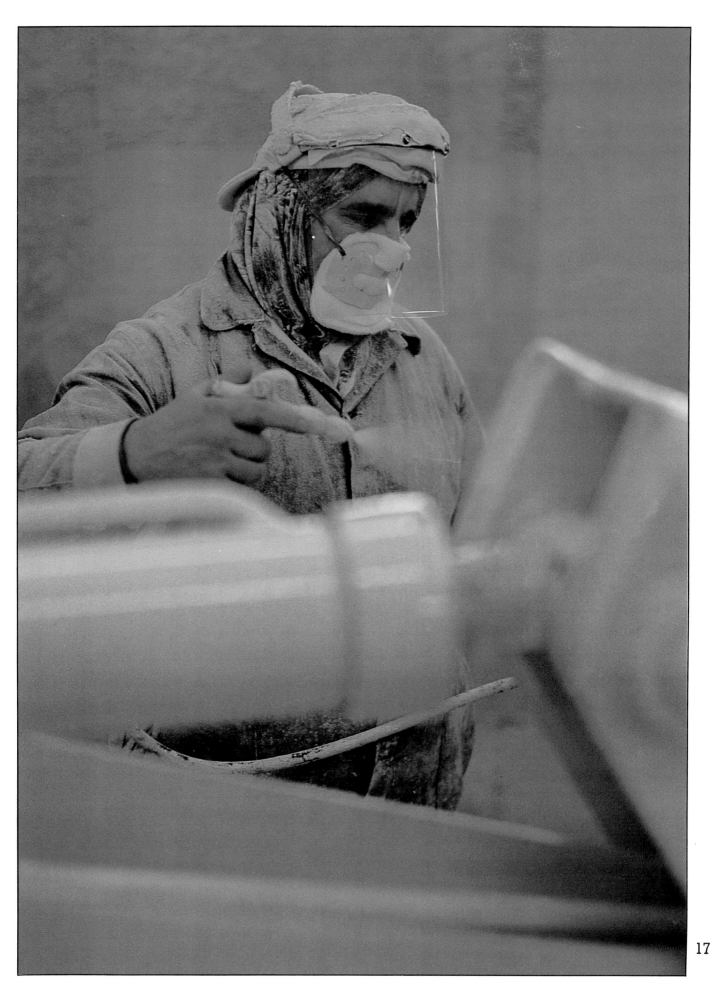

Spray painters use masks to protect them from dangerous chemicals

CRYSTALS

We have seen how to separate salt from a salt solution. If you look at this salt under a microscope, you can see that each grain of salt is a perfect cube. The cubes form naturally as the salt comes out of solution. They are called salt "crystals." All salt crystals are the same shape, although they may be different sizes.

Many chemicals form crystals. Sugar makes crystals and so does water vapor when it turns to frost or snow. Each of these crystals has its own particular shape. Most rocks are made up of crystals of chemical compounds called "minerals." For example, granite is made up of crystals of "quartz," "feldspar" and "mica." Crystals of sapphire, diamond or emerald may be made into jewelry. They are all examples of crystals we call "gems."

Salt crystals

Salt is made up of an equal number of sodium and chlorine atoms. When salt is in solution, these atoms are far apart. But as the water evaporates, the atoms get close together. They always arrange themselves in the same way. This arrangement, called a "crystal lattice," gives the salt its cubic shape.

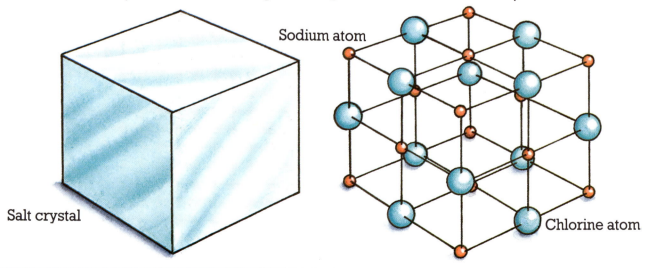

Salt crystal

Sodium atom

Chlorine atom

CARBON

Carbon is an element: it is made up of carbon atoms only. But these atoms can arrange themselves in a number of ways to form several different types of carbon crystals. For example, charcoal is a soft black substance that can be used for drawing or may be burned as a fuel; graphite is harder and is used to make the "lead" in pencils. Surprisingly, diamonds are also pure carbon! Unlike charcoal and graphite, diamonds are extremely rare. They are used to make highly priced jewelry, and they also have industrial uses. Diamond is the hardest substance known and can be shaped to make cutting tools.

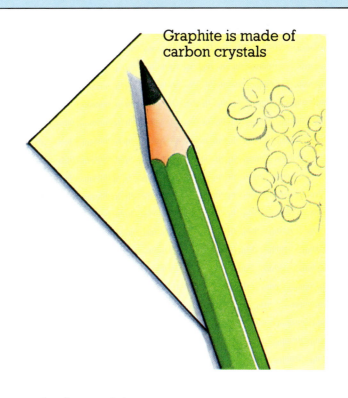

Graphite is made of carbon crystals

Diamond crystals can be cut and polished to make beautiful gemstones

ACIDS AND ALKALIS

Some chemicals can be described as acids or alkalis. Vinegar, lemon juice and sour milk are all weak acids. They all have a similar sharp, sour taste. Alkalis are very different from acids. They taste bitter and feel soapy. Oven cleaner, baking soda and toothpaste are all alkalis.

Our stomachs contain a solution of an acid called "hydrochloric acid." This acid kills some of the bacteria in our food and helps us to digest our meals. But too much acid in the stomach causes indigestion. Medicines used to cure stomach pains are often alkalis. When you mix an alkali with an acid, you make a solution that is "neutral" – neither acid nor alkaline. Since many plants thrive in a soil that is not very acid, farmers and gardeners may add lime to the soil. Lime (an alkali) "neutralizes" soil that is too acid.

Indicators

An "indicator," such as litmus, is a substance that changes color when it is mixed with an acid or an alkali. When litmus paper is dipped into lemon juice, it turns red. Stomach medicine turns it blue. When the acid and the alkali are mixed, a neutral solution is formed which does not color the litmus.

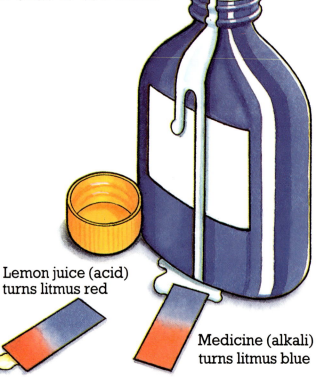

Lemon juice (acid) turns litmus red

Medicine (alkali) turns litmus blue

Firemen use an alkali to neutralize acid leaking from a tanker

CHEMICALS IN THE AIR

Air is a mixture. It contains many gases including nitrogen, oxygen and carbon dioxide. Nitrogen can combine with other elements to make compounds called "proteins." Plants and animals need proteins to help them grow. They also need oxygen to breathe. At the top of a mountain, there is less air than at the bottom – and so less oxygen. For this reason, mountain climbers sometimes need to take extra oxygen with them.

Plants use carbon dioxide. In sunlight, plants grow by combining carbon dioxide and water to produce more of the chemicals of which they are made. Though the gases in the air are being used all the time, they never run out! The diagram below will help you understand why.

The Gas Cycle

We take oxygen from the air, but put back carbon dioxide – plants need carbon dioxide and, during the day, get rid of their oxygen. Plant and animal bodies contain nitrogen. When they die, this nitrogen returns to the air or soil.

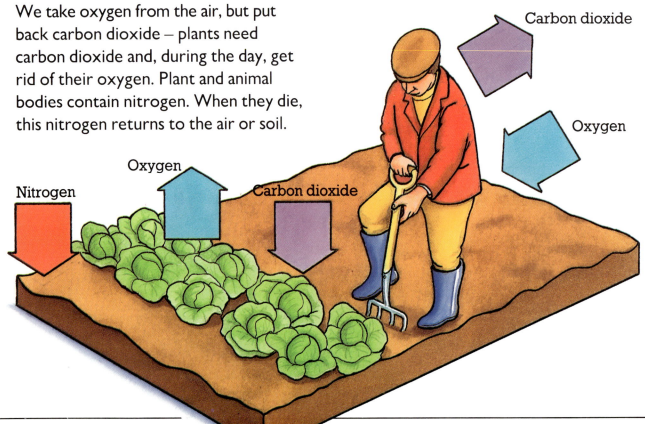

Carbon dioxide

Oxygen

Oxygen

Nitrogen

Carbon dioxide

At high altitudes, climbers wear oxygen masks to help them breathe

CHEMICALS FROM OIL

Crude oil is a thick, black liquid found deep under the Earth's surface. It was formed millions of years ago from the bodies of tiny animals and plants which lived in the sea. Crude oil is of little use as it is. But this liquid is really a mixture of several liquids which are very useful.

Crude oil is pumped up to the Earth's surface and is piped to a refinery. Here the different liquids are separated from each other. Some of the liquids, such as gasoline and kerosene, can be used as fuels. Others are changed chemically to produce compounds, such as plastics and waxes. Many of the things we use every day contain chemicals that come from oil. You can see some of them in the photograph below.

Many things can be made from plastic, for example clothes, shoes and toys

Each liquid chemical boils at a different temperature. The temperature at which it boils is called its "boiling point." When crude oil is heated at the refinery, its temperature slowly rises. The liquid with the lowest boiling point is the first one to boil and form a gas. This gas rises upward, then cools back to a liquid and is collected. As the heating continues, the liquids are separated and collected one by one. The last liquid to be collected is the one with the highest boiling point. This process of separation is called "distillation."

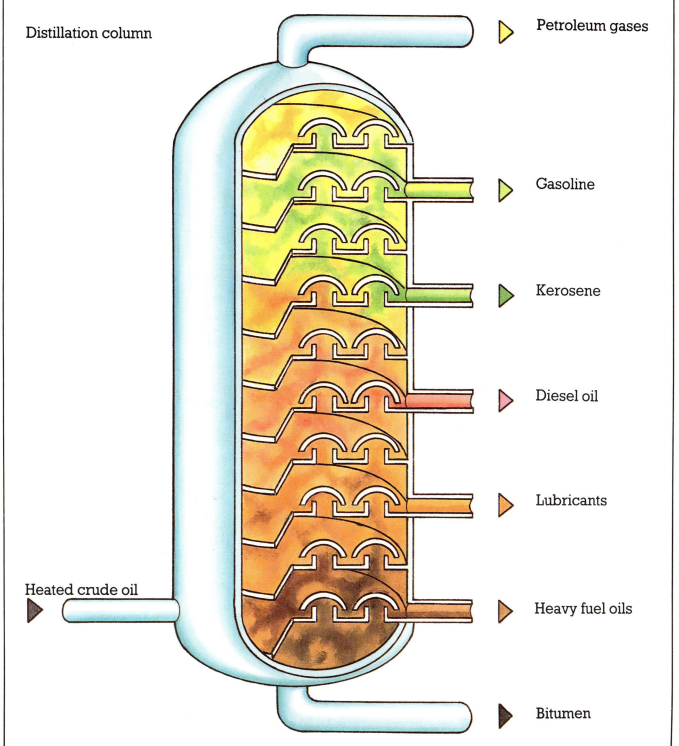

Distillation column

Petroleum gases

Gasoline

Kerosene

Diesel oil

Lubricants

Heated crude oil

Heavy fuel oils

Bitumen

People have always used natural chemicals in their daily lives. Vegetable dyes are used to color wool and cloth or to make paint. Other chemicals from plants have been used as medicines. Originally, drugs such as penicillin were made from molds grown naturally. Today, most of our medicines, for example painkillers, are artificially produced.

Scientists have produced chemicals to help the farmer. Fertilizers, spread on the fields, make crops more plentiful and strong. Chemicals called "pesticides" can be used to kill insects that damage crops. Although chemicals are used to improve our lives, many may be harmful too. For this reason, chemicals are developed and tested in laboratories before they are used.

Many diseases can be treated by drugs made from artificial chemicals

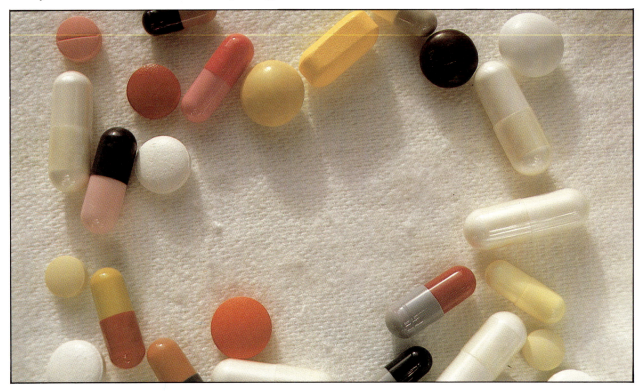

Pesticides are sprayed on crops to protect them from being eaten by insects

Warning
Chemicals can be dangerous. Ask a grown-up to help you choose safe ones for your test.

Red cabbage, like many other plant materials, contains a colored chemical that acts as an indicator. The purple dye from the cabbage turns red in acids and green in alkalis. Make your own indicator and find out which of the everyday chemicals you have at home are acids or alkalis.

What you need

Blotting paper

Red cabbage

Ask a grown-up to boil some cabbage leaves in water. The dye from the cabbage will turn the water purple.

When the solution has cooled, you can pour it into a container. Leave the cabbage leaves in the pan — you do not need them.

Dip strips of white blotting paper into the indicator solution. When they are soaked in dye leave them to dry.

Use your indicator paper to test any liquids you may have. (You can also test solids dissolved in water.) Just place a few drops of each chemical onto a fresh piece of indicator paper. Record your results on a chart — like the one in the diagram.

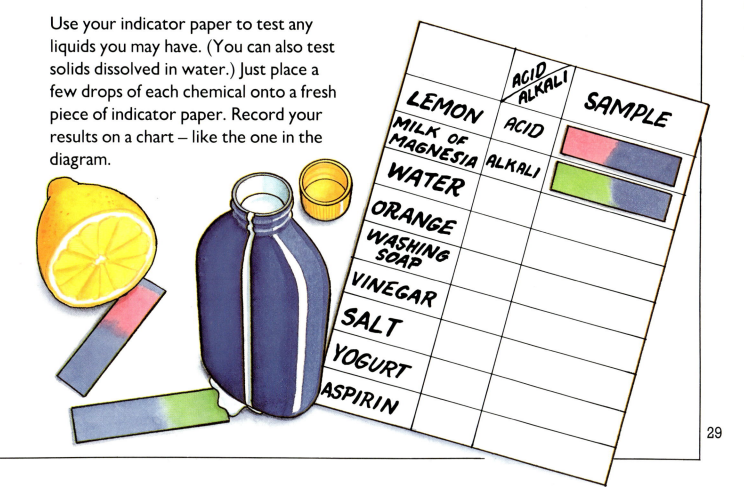

	ACID / ALKALI	SAMPLE
LEMON	ACID	
MILK OF MAGNESIA	ALKALI	
WATER		
ORANGE		
WASHING SOAP		
VINEGAR		
SALT		
YOGURT		
ASPIRIN		

MORE ABOUT CHEMICALS

Physical change

Iron filings and sulfur, both elements, can be mixed together. However, the iron filings can be easily separated from the mixture as they are attracted by a magnet. This is an example of a physical change. In a physical change, the material changes only its appearance. It is easy to reverse the change and get the original material back again because no new substances are formed.

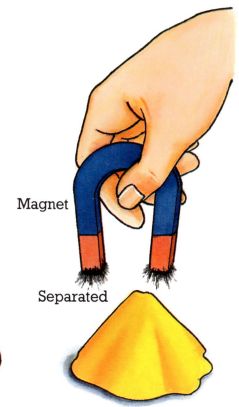

Magnet

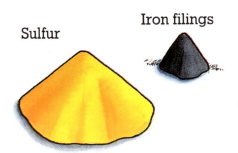

Sulfur

Iron filings

Mixed together

Separated

Chemical change

Most of the chemicals around us exist as mixtures of compounds; for example, eggs and bread are mixtures of compounds. When mixtures like these are heated, new compounds are formed; the foods change their taste, texture and appearance. This is because a chemical change – or reaction – has taken place. We cannot undo this change in a simple way. Only complex chemical processes can reverse a chemical change. We say that chemical changes are "irreversible."

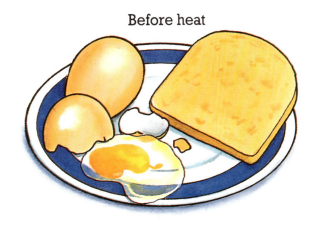

Before heat

After heat

GLOSSARY

Atom
A tiny particle. It is the smallest part of an element that can exist and still have all the characteristics of that element. It is the smallest unit of matter that can take part in a chemical change.

Compound
A substance consisting of two or more elements joined together. It cannot be broken down by physical changes.

Crystal lattice
The regular arrangement of atoms in a solid compound which gives it its characteristic shape.

Detergent
A substance that can be used to remove dirt and grease. Detergents are often manmade.

Diffusion
The gradual spreading of one material into another. Diffusion is quick in gases, slower in liquids and very slow in solids.

Dye
A colored substance that can be firmly fixed to another substance. Generally, it will not be removed by water or detergents.

Element
A substance that cannot be split into anything simpler by a chemical process, e.g., iron, oxygen.

Litmus
A purple dye obtained from a type of plant called a lichen. It acts as an indicator.

Mixture
Two or more substances together that can be separated by simple physical means.

Molecule
A molecule is the smallest part of an element or compound that can exist on its own and still have all the characteristics of that element or compound. Molecules of elements have one atom or two or more different atoms, those of compounds have two or more different atoms.

Plastics
Compounds that contain carbon and whose molecules usually exist in long chains. Heat and/or pressure are involved in their manufacture.

Property
A characteristic that describes how a substance appears or behaves under certain conditions.

Reaction
The events that take place when two substances act on each other to produce new compounds.

Solution
When a solid, or a gas, dissolves in a liquid, we say it forms a solution.

INDEX

Photographic Credits:
Cover, contents page, title page and
pages 11, 17 and 26; Tony Stone: page 6;
Topham: page 7; Picturepoint: page 9;
Bruce Colman: pages 13, 19, 21 and 24;
Zefa: page 15; Ardea: page 23; John
Cleare (Mountain Camera): page 27;
Camerapix Hutchinson.

PRINTED IN BELGIUM BY
proost
INTERNATIONAL BOOK PRODUCTION